FEELINGS IN PARADISE.

Paradise Dickinson

Presentation by *BookLeaf Publishing*

Web: www.bookleafpub.com

E-mail: info@bookleafpub.com

ISBN: 9789357748612

First edition 2023

ACKNOWLEDGEMENT

I am a lone soul and truthfully, I am not one to acknowledge people either. Hell, it's hard enough for me to just acknowledge my own feelings as it is. However, there are a handful of people that I am beyond grateful and thankful for.

First, I want to thank God, because without him I would not be here, and I would not have experienced any of the trials, tribulations, lessons and blessings within this lifetime he so graciously gives me. I also would not know what love truly is, as his love has never failed me.

Second, I want to thank my mother, Angela and my father, Frank because without you both, I also would not be here on this earth. I'd still be a soul waiting to incarnate into a family. I'd like to say we chose each other for this lifetime, and for that, I am forever thankful and grateful. I love you both unconditionally.

Third, I want to thank my two daughters, Harper and Havana plus my children in heaven and my future children. Without you all, I wouldn't be a mother. One of the very first dreams I ever wanted for my life, was to be a mother, so I could shower you all with the love that I never got growing up. I wanted to show you exactly what unconditional love feels like, and I will continue everyday doing just that. You are THE greatest blessing God has ever given me. I am forever thankful and grateful you guys choosing me to be your mother. I love you all unconditionally.

Fourth, I want to thank my former therapist, Michael. You are an absolute angel. You never gave up on me, you always pushed me to be better and do better. You never made me feel small or worthless like most people in my life, in-fact you made me feel big and worthy. You continuously supported my dreams and my decisions, even when I KNOW some of my decisions you didn't like. For that, I am forever thankful and grateful. I love you unconditionally.

Fifth, I want to thank Renee and Lisa for supporting me and showing me who I truly am on a soul level and reminding me of the magic that was inside me all along just waiting to be released out onto this earth. I love you both unconditionally.

Twenty second and longer hugs to you all and everyone else in this world.

water.

Water everywhere.
Leave me alone, get out of my ear.

Water here. Water there.
Water in my ear and hair.

Drowning out the voices and the pain,
I can't hear you mom & dad, it's dark down here,
what did you say?

Be gone, be lost, don't even bother making a
splash.
No one seems to care if I even last.
SPLISH AND SPLASH.

Water is everywhere like the big wide ocean.
Miles across the country, I feel so wide open.
Lost and confused, I think I have the blues.

Some days are bright.
Some days are dark.
Some days I just want to make art.
Other days, I just want to dart.

Over here or over there,

Please God, give me a breath of fresh air.
I think I am starting to drown as I watch the sun
go down.

Water here. Water there.
Water filling my lungs as I gasp for air.
I have nothing left to spare.

Water here. Water there.
Water seems to be everywhere.

Help, help, help, I need out of here.
The waves won't disappear.
Pulling me under with no despair.
Please mom and dad, why did you put me here?

little bird.

Fly away little bird.
As fast as you can little bird.
Don't look back little bird.
Come back little bird.
Fly away little bird.
Don't come back little bird.

In the sky, you fly high.
In the sky, you fly high.
In the sky, you fly high.
Crashing down.
Crashing down.
Coming down.
Coming down.
Fallen down.
Little bird down, on the ground.

On the ground, there you lay.
Begging, Hoping, Praying for another day.
On the ground, there you lay.
Pull yourself together, it will be okay.

Get up little bird.
Stand tall, little bird.
Smile little bird.

Grab my hand little bird.
Fly away little bird.
As fast as you can little bird.
And never look back little bird.

Fly.
And Fly.
And fly.
Spread your wings and keep flying.
Far away, fly away, I told you, you'd be okay.
Little bird, you made it to another day.
Let's Pray.

orange hue.

In the first-row church pew, I can still feel you.
The energetic orange hue, shinning from behind
my view.

In the first-row church pew, I cannot see you,
only feel you.
Daddy preaches and now I feel brand-new.
I believe this is a fucking breakthrough.

In the first-row church pew, it feels like I'm
waiting for an interview.
In the first-row church pew, I just want you to
pursue.
In the first-row church pew, your orange hue is
blocking my view.

I know this is all taboo.
But I really want to hold your hand, and say I
DO.
Every time I think of you, I get lost in your
orange hue.

rainbow.

Are you brown or are you peach?
Why do we always have to compete?

My team, your team, their team.
I think I might fucking scream.

Purple. Red. Blue. And Gold.
Why is the world so fucking cold?

Orange. Yellow. Silver. And Green.
Get out of your fucking phone screen.
Put it down, the tv remote too.
Your little ones are watching you.

Grab my hand and please give me a hug too.
I just want to make the world brand-new.

If we love, we will fit like, a glove.
So be an example and go light your candle.
Stop neglecting your hippocampal.

family.

Family isn't always blood; it can be your pastor
and friends too.
Although I love my blood family, all the way to
the moon.

But sometimes it's okay to undue the family you
once knew.
To wash them all away, with nothing but
shampoo.
Simply, all because you, finally fucking outgrew.

I will never forget the ones that birthed and
conditioned me.
Truly, I am thankful for the curse you have given
me.

But now it's time to enjoy my new family.
For you are forgiven with my dearest sympathy.

time to live.

You touch me but I don't touch you.
I'm frozen in this dark back bedroom.

Dazed. Lost. And confused.
Not really sure what to do.

Is this right?
Or is this wrong?
I am starting to feel like I don't belong.

You get angry when I try to scream.
Could this all be just a dream?

I realize now it's not a dream.
You cover my mouth while I try to scream.

I close my eyes, praying to the skies.
Wishing and hoping you'd get out of between
my thighs.

You touch me, but I don't touch you.
I wish you knew how much I grew.

And it's time now to forgive, all because it's time
to live.

ocean whale.

Sitting by the ocean, listening to the sound of the
waves.
I can get lost in their sirens for days.
Splish and splash while the waves crash.
Did I just see a mermaid jump over the pass?

I must be dreaming because the sun is beaming
and gleaming.
So, I'll close my eyes because I don't want to tell
any lies.
I only heard about the tales, talking about their
glistening, glowing scales.
Shinny and colorful. Vibrant and pale.
Fuck! It must have been a whale.

Wait a minute, a whale is too big.
I know what I saw, I am not a kid.
Although kids see the truth, they just never have
any proof.
I know first-hand because I once knew a man.

H.Melville was his name. He wrote a book and
got some fame.
So, I'll say it again and maybe we'll still be
friends.

I was sitting by the ocean, listening to the sound of the waves.
I saw a mermaid and got lost in the ocean daze.

the devil.

The devil.
You are a rebel.
You come in any form you want.
You come in any color you want.
You will become anything when you're on the
hunt.

You will kick us down when we're already on
the ground.
You will mash our face right in the same place.
You will extend your hand while making another
command.
You will give us a hug while you pull the rug.

The devil.
You are a fucking rebel.

You will tell us you love us while you shove us.
You will say you're sorry while you buy us a
ferrari.
You will say we're pretty and still make us feel
itty-bitty.
You will cuddle us just to muddle us.

You are the devil, you are a fucking rebel.

And now you are done throwing your fucking pebble.

So, you can go back to your fucking hell hole.

airport eyes.

Stopped by security, I just want security.
Voices and people all around.
Fuck, I spilt my coffee on the ground.
Whispers, cries, and laughs.
Long stares and broken paths.

Your friend won't stop talking.
And you won't stop gawking.
Your beautiful brown eyes intertwined with
mine.
Your mask is up, how do you drink from your
cup?
Your soul, my soul, we could've been whole.
Your heart, my heart, together we could've made
art.

Your airport eyes, I can still feel them in the
skies.
You said you write poems and that you can make
me moan.
But that's not what I need, you're not planting a
seed.
So you make me plead, seven long months down
on my knees.

I just wanted your love, I know you felt it
through my hug.
I told you I loved you, I am not above you.
Your airport eyes had me hypnotized.
I was mesmerized by all your lies.
Your airport eyes gave a real good disguise.

You said your hearts broken, I never wanted to
be your token.
I grabbed your hand and tried to make you, my
man.
We could've been each other's fan, I used to call
you Dan.
Your airport eyes, had me lost in the skies.

The sun, he told me yes, but the moon, she told
me no.
When its back and forth, that's when I knew it
was warped.
Your airport eyes are now forever imprinted into
mine.
But now I am done because you pulled the gun.
Your brown eyes, you can keep all your big and
white lies.
You had your chance, we never got to dance.
I choose me, so I can be free.
You have the key, now please leave me be.

you should be mine.

You should be mine; I don't want to cross the
line.
I know you're the one, I don't mean to jump the
gun.
I knew it when our eyes locked, you stopped the
clock.
I can wait but please don't be late.
We already set the weddin' date.

Your soul and my soul, together we are whole.
You're not like the rest; you're putting me
through a test.
Your kids and my kids, together they're our kids.
I know you're confused, so let me be your muse.

She's not the one, she already pulled the gun.
You know this, you cannot dismiss.
She's trying to pull you into the abyss.
There's no time to reminisce.

But when I am not with you, damn do I miss
you.
I know you're the one, so let's make this fun.
Fuck it, let's give it a run, I will never pull the
gun.

You know I am the one.

Together we're legends, they know it in heaven.
Now it's eleven o' seven, now let's get to our
weddin'.

ohio.

Black hole, black hole, I see a mole.
Black hole, black hole, you're such a troll.
Black hole, black hole, I rather pay a toll.

Black hole, Black hole, this place doesn't feel
whole.
Black hole, black hole, you're trying to take
control.
Black hole, black hole, you're trying to consume
my soul.

Black hole, black hole, you're not stopping my
goal.
Black hole, black hole, I am not stepping on
your coal.
Black hole, black hole, Ohio is a hell hole.

therapy.

I used to be scared of me until I got help from therapy.
So much has happened, I'm sure you can imagine.

When I was weak, Michael helped me get on my feet.
Twice a week, we would usually meet until the cycle was complete.

He showed me I am enough and that I am tough.
I am as tough as a nail; I could probably sail—

Out into the deep blue ocean, away from all this commotion.
Where I can be free to finally be me.

I'll fly with the bees out into the seas.
I'm finally free! Damn, it feels good to be me.

soul sister.

Sisters but you guys come from different misses
and misters.
You came into each other's lives in the midst of
a twister.

You never dissed her or dismissed her.
You only missed her.
She's your soul sister.

Nutritional love. Never conditional love.
Decisional love. Never propositional love.
Pure and genuine, unconditional love.

Never collisional or divisional love. Just
medicinal love.
Sisters. That's your soul, sister.

generalized anxiety disorder

You were always so mad.
You were always so bad.

You were always so sad.
And now I got extreme GAD.

You never showed any fad, not even a tad.
Even though you're my dad, you were never rad.

I wish you were glad and would've come to my
grad.
You're still my number one dad, even when
you're mad.

sunflowers.

Sunflowers have magical powers.
I can stare at them for hours.

Long green stems with petals looking like
yellow gems.
Shinning in the Sun, never making me want to
pull a gun.

Meaning longevity and they're a friend of me.
Brightening my mood even when they're food.

Nourishing the earth, it really gives me worth.
Even in solidarity, they bring me clarity.

Sunflowers empower.
They are my favorite flower.

It's the witching hour, I shall not cower.
I will build a tower and watch you all scour.

Man, look at those sunflowers we just
encountered.
Now I have magical powers and not just flowers.

best friend.

Best friends in high school, how could you be so cruel?
You knew you were my enemy and you still befriended me.

I thought we were cool; damn I was such a fool.
We were two peas in a pod even though you were on the cheer squad.

You put on a facade; you really did your job.
When you hit me, it felt like a rod, you really made me nod.

You were such a snob; did you even know God?
I prayed for your healing way past the ceiling.

But it's not my business so I'll be with the quickness.
I give you my forgiveness even in your sickness.

Because you were my best friend, I'll pray you transcend and ascend.
And maybe one day we will mend and put this all to an end.

roy.

You came into my life after I found Christ.
He got taken so quick; it was so swift.

I'll never forget the ring and how it made me
scream.
But when I walked through the door, I couldn't
have asked for more.

You came right up and then you filled my cup.
I knew our time was short, but I couldn't abort.

I was all in as soon as you made my heart spin.
Your four giant paws busted down my rock-solid
walls.

I could feel your pain just as much as mine.
I could feel your love and how it was on
borrowed time.

Your starred into my soul and you made me feel
whole.
Even your slobbery drool never had any rules.

Every time I was down, you made sure to
always come around.

And I always made sure you were fed even
when I couldn't get out of our bed.

You never left my side, you made sure to stay
for the ride.
Even in our end of times, I made sure you were
always mine.

My birthday is here, I didn't expect any tears.
One and a half years wasn't enough, damn this is
tough.

We were heading to the vet; I didn't expect to
lose my pet.
It was just supposed to be shots, but then the
clock stopped and I was congested into knots.

Pulling the plug after I gave you your final hug.
But I knew it was time, damn I wish you were
still mine.

Everyday I think about you, I won't forget about
you.
You'll never be replaced, not even in space.

Your name is Roy, and you were so full of joy.
So I'll carry our memories and you'll always be
a friend of me.

baby blue.

Well hello there, baby blue.
Oh look! I'm wearing you too.

I walked in, there you glanced.
Oh how, I wish we could dance.

I got your message.
Loud and clear.
This is a fucking night-mare.

I was prepared with a speech.
I prepared for at least a week.

Couldn't you just let me preach?
Instead, you were without-reach.

I've been yearning for your love.
I know, you know, we fit like a glove.

Unless I was fooled again, yet again…
Damn! When is this going to end?

I have wanted love ever since I was ten.
Probably because of all, the men.

But they weren't men, they were sick.
They were way fucking-worse.

They harmed me sexually and physically.
You harmed me whole-heartedly, neglected-ly.

But when you took your glance.
Oh how, my heart fucking-danced.

Skipped a beat, a little flutter.
You too look, like, a lot of clutter.

You know, I know, you could do better.
Are you feeling a little under the, weather?

Let me hold you, just one time.
Oh how, I wish, you were mine.

Let me smooth your mind.
I'm not trying to commit any crime.

Don't you think we are running out of time?
Would you like a glass of wine?

Just one life. Why not live it?
Or would you just rather quit it?

At least then, I'd be in the baby blue sky.

And not feel it on the inside.

One last time, would you be mine?
Just one time.

may showers.

Shattered vases and broken glasses.
I think I see too many fucking asses.

My head is like a maze.
I'm lost in a fucking daze.

It showers in the month of May.
He took you away.

It showers in the month of May.
I just want to run away.

It showers in the month of May.
They say it'll be okay.

I'm losing track of days.
They say that it's just a phase.

Shattered vases and broken fasteners.
I think she's got a phat ass on her.

I just want another glass in here.
Ima make it shower like May up in here.

www.ingramcontent.com/pod-product-compliance
Lightning Source LLC
La Vergne TN
LVHW010949200726
843509LV00013B/2336